Life Without Limits

Life Without *Limits*

THINK~BELIEVE~DECREE

52 Biblical Principles
To Reach Your Prophetic Destiny

Tiffany K. Jordan

Life Without Limits ~ Think Believe Decree

Published by Covenant Connection

Copyright © 2014 Tiffany K. Jordan

All Rights Reserved
ISBN: 978-0-9960251-0-2

Print Edition

Unless otherwise stated all Scripture quotations come from the King James version of the Bible

**For more information about Covenant Connection,
please call 630-426-9507**

**Or write to us at:
380 East St. Charles #231
Lombard, IL 60148**

Visit our websites:
www.covenantconnectioncorp.com
www.tiffanyjordanministries.org

Please also include your prayer request.

CONTENTS

ACKNOWLEDGEMENTS

I have been blessed with the ability to write this book and foremost, I thank God for giving me these principles along with His guidance in every step.

For my beautiful children Shondasia and Corinthia, I am grateful. They have been a major contribution to the passion for my call and living life by faith. This came because of my desire to demonstrate to them that God is faithful, and that His Word partnered with both faith and perseverance pays off no matter what it looks like.

To my Pastors and Spiritual Parents, Drs. Bill and Veronica Winston, you are amazing and it has been an honor to be connected to the vision of our church and serve within it for many years. You have transformed my life forever by your teachings and demonstration of God's Word. As a result, I have done things I never thought was possible. Daily I pray for you and thank God for the mark you have made upon my life.

In addition, I am thankful for every intercessor that prayed and believed God with me; through intercession you acted as a midwife, as I birthed this book into being.

Finally I give thanks for Chief Jimmy Delano who prophesied to me with specific details regarding the birth of this book. I believe because of the prophecy a scribal anointing was activated that allowed me to transcribe this book. Truly a supernatural endowment came upon me and I am forever grateful to you sir. Thank you for your obedience.

May God richly bless each of these extraordinary people!

FOREWORD
By Chief Jimmy G. Delano

If you have not met the author Minister Tiffany Jordan, after having read *"Life Without Limits"* you would have been exposed to a remarkable individual. Those of us that know her, will acknowledge that this is a subject that she is gifted to write about.

This book is based on a powerful idea that tackles 52 biblical principles to reach the readers prophetic destiny, that is central to our Christian faith and growth. It is timely writing as we are in a time where supernatural is a requirement every day in our Christian lives.

One by one, 52 biblical principles: favor, wisdom, knowledge etc. receives prophetic treatment. Every principle the author writes about have a ring of prophetic decree, abated by a crisp of simple style.

By embracing God's revelation in each of these principles, the commentary of each bible passage gives the reader a fresh revelation and perspective of the Kingdom of God's principles. It renews the reader's courage and provides a better understanding of our LORD'S will in our lives.

I identify with this book, as I believe there is a surprising treasure in each of the 52 principles. All of them are biblical, and it is recommended to the readers to read, memorize and meditate on each principle every day of the 52 weeks of the year.

Minister Tiffany is a gifted communicator and writer. She brings her prophetic gifts and creativity to the book transforming each principle with her commentary and prophetic decree. They are Holy potentials that are spoken into the reader's life. Your mind will be elevated and you will think like God, which will lead to supernatural results.

My prayer is as you read this book your faith will be birthed, coming fully alive into your hearts to believe God for his promises.

You will note that I have no hesitation in recommending this book for ALL, regardless of background. It should embolden, encourage, and reveal God's word. This book will be an asset for you to own and a gift for you to give to many others.

— **Chief Jimmy G. Delano**

Delano is a man of God and teacher of the word who studied Theology at Oxford University, Oxford, England. He is the author of *"THANKING GOD"*, which was published in 2013. He is also the President of **Corporate Prayer Room** (CPR), a non-denominational International prayer ministry and of **HARMONY international Group**, which markets consumer goods into over 20 countries of the world. In 2008 the USA Congress awarded him a Certificate of Special Congressional Recognition for outstanding and invaluable service. For further information email: gboyegadelano@aol.com

HOW TO USE THIS BOOK

This is a prophetic book that was produced through a prophetic Word from the Lord where each word came as a download. Be sure to pay close attention because each principle shall activate you to propel in purpose. This book is designed to renew your mind and shift you into higher measures of the anointing. Every principle is biblical and as you individually meditate them according to the season you are in, your mind will be elevated to think as God does and produce supernatural results.

I believe that the grace that rested on me to write this book will also come upon those that read it. You will be anointed to do all that God has called you to do. A spirit of acceleration will be your portion and your life will never be the same. Your ability to meditate, believe and act on the principles is what matters not your background, age, or current circumstances.

Since it is 52 weeks in a year, this book has 52 principles. If you meditate a principle per week, you shall have a supernatural year, every year. This book is not to be read once but for each and every year of your life. By doing this week by week you shall grow in strength, effectiveness, and influence. You will be activated to tap into your power, and you shall live a life WITHOUT LIMITS!

THE ORDER OF THINGS

THINK ~ Proverbs 23:7(a) "For as he thinketh in his heart, so is he."

The concept is to renew our minds so that our thinking lines up with the Word of God.

BELIEVE ~ Mark 9:23 "Jesus said unto him, If thou canst believe, all things are possible to him that believeth.

We must believe that the Word of God is ultimate truth, in order to have the manifestation in our lives. Everything else must be considered a lie.

DECREE ~ Job 22:28 (a) "Thou shalt also decree a thing, and it shall be established unto thee:"

We must boldly declare what is ours by faith, before we have any evidence of it. Confession brings forth possession!

THE PRINCIPLES

- PRINCIPLE ONE -

PEACE

Philippians 4:6-7

6 Be careful for nothing; but in every thing by prayer and supplication with thanksgiving let your requests be made known unto God.

7 And the **peace** of God, which passeth all understanding, shall keep your hearts and minds through Christ Jesus.

Your peace is important. Never let anything or anyone remove it. Find a place to focus on God and his goodness. Clear your mind and pray unto to the Lord that your peace be restored in the midst of every circumstance. God's peace shall keep your heart and mind sound. Remove anything including relationships from your life and environment that are toxic and cause your peace to be compromised. This is non-negotiable.

Prophetic Decree

The peace of God is my portion. I take whatever measures are necessary, to maintain God's peace in my life. His peace keeps my heart & mind through Christ Jesus. I do not allow anything to steal the peace that God has provided for me. My peace is sustained because my mind is fixed on Him.

- PRINCIPLE TWO -
RENEW YOUR MIND

Romans 12:2

And be not conformed to this world: but be ye transformed by the **renewing of your mind**, that ye may prove what is that good, and acceptable, and perfect, will of God.

Your mind is the place where the enemy likes to send suggestive thoughts. It is your responsibility to renew it to God's Word. Replace any ungodly thoughts with God's Word the minute you have them. Even though we are born again, our minds must be renewed. God has things that He wants to deliver to us, however, we must think on a higher level, beyond what our experiences, environments and teachers have programmed us to think. Renew your mind by meditating on God's Word daily. The changes will be notable in your life, and undeniable.

Prophetic Decree

I decide today to meditate God's Word daily. My mind is being renewed and my life is being transformed. I will not conform to this world, but I am walking out the good and acceptable perfect will of God for my life by faith.

- PRINCIPLE THREE -
PROMOTION

Psalm 75:6

For **promotion** cometh neither from the east, nor from the west, nor from the south.

Trust God to promote you. Make sure that you are prepared to walk in the promotion that He will bring your way. God desires that His people always progress and not be stagnant. Prepare, expect and receive his promotion as you are being positioned to go higher. You shall be lifted up to the glory of God. Do not look to man, for even if man announces it, know that it came from the Lord and He should receive all the glory for it.

Prophetic Decree

I understand that promotion comes from God; therefore, I position myself to receive increase in every area of my life. I do what is necessary to receive from God the promotion that I have the capacity to possess. I expect promotion and I walk toward it, without hesitation.

- PRINCIPLE FOUR -
LEADERSHIP

Mark 10:44

And whosoever of you will be the chiefest, shall be **servant of all.**

A True Leader Leads by Example!

Leading by example is a great motivator to all of those that will come along side you and assist you in your endeavors. As a leader, you cannot expect your team to do what you are not willing to do. Leaders may do more than the team, but the team will develop a greater level of respect for them. A leader that doesn't just talk, but does above and beyond will be honored.

Prophetic Decree

I am a leader that leads by example. I set a standard of excellence and work together with my team to achieve the highest results. We know that working together produces the best fruit. I am an extraordinary leader.

Visionary

- PRINCIPLE FIVE -

FAVOR

Luke 2:52

And Jesus increased in wisdom and stature, and in **favour** with God and man.

Expect the favor of God to be upon you daily as you are transacting business and communicating with people. God has already gone before you, make sure to declare it and expect it everywhere you go. His favor will cause everything you need and desire to line up and be granted unto you. The favor of God will literally change the rules and regulations of a system to accommodate your Kingdom assignment.

Prophetic Decree

I expect God's favor to go before me daily. I am favored of God and man. His favor opens up doors for me and causes me to have undeniable blessings bestowed upon me. I declare that I walk in God's divine favor every day of my life. I am blessed and highly favored.

- PRINCIPLE SIX -
WISDOM

James 1:5

If any of you lack **wisdom**, let him ask of God, that giveth to all men liberally, and upbraideth not; and it shall be given him.

Daily ask God for His wisdom and He will give it to you. We can have knowledge, but the wisdom of God cannot be denied or resisted. Consistently we want to have God's wisdom flowing to us, through our minds, and out of our mouths; whether we are conducting business or dealing with people and situations. God's wisdom in you will trigger creativity from you.

Prophetic Decree

Father I ask you for the wisdom that is from above. I declare every time I open my mouth your wisdom comes forth. I decree that I have wisdom in business, finances, relationships, family, health, and every other area of my life. I receive and walk in God's wisdom today and forever more.

- PRINCIPLE SEVEN -

GIVING

Luke 6:38

Give, and it shall be given unto you; good measure, pressed down, shaken together, and running over, shall men give into your bosom. For with the same measure that ye mete withal it shall be measured to you again.

First, make a lifestyle of being not just a giver, but a cheerful one. God has blessed you to be a blessing. Secondly, be sure that your tithe consists of all income and profit earned. Lastly, sow seed on purpose and expect a harvest because God is faithful to not just return the seed, but the harvest also in multiplied measure.

Prophetic Decree

I decree that I am a cheerful giver and therefore I reap a bountiful harvest. I give and it is given unto me good measure, pressed down shaken together and running over, men give unto my bosom. I consistently give, and I am abundantly replenished.

- PRINCIPLE EIGHT -

FEAR

II Timothy 1:7

For God hath not given us the spirit of **fear**; but of power, and of love, and of a sound mind.

Fear opens the door to limitations and frustration. You cannot be in faith and fear at the same time. Deal with any area where there is fear. Face it because usually on the other side of it is an amazing discovery of blessing, and a gift that will produce much increase.

Prophetic Decree

Today I renounce all fear in my life. I rebuke the spirit of fear in Jesus name, and receive boldness. From this day forward, I will face any area where there was fear head on. I am more than a conqueror and no fear lives here. I am bold and courageous.

- PRINCIPLE NINE -
KNOWLEDGE

Hosea 4:6a

My people are destroyed for lack of **knowledge**...

Money, people, family, etc. is not your problem.
Knowledge is essential. In the Kingdom it is
important to have revelation knowledge to add to
the natural knowledge that we get from books and
experiences. God's power added produces the
supernatural in our lives. Invest in natural and
spiritual knowledge by reading natural books and the
Word of God daily.

Prophetic Decree

I know that no person on this is earth is my
problem. I renounce blaming, and commit myself to
gaining knowledge naturally and spiritually. I grow in
knowledge daily; I meditate the word, read books,
and increase in the knowledge of God's perfect will.

EXPECTATION

Psalm 62:5

My soul, wait thou only upon God; for my
expectation is from him.

What are you expecting? Who are you expecting it
from? Our expectation must be in the Lord. He
alone will bring things to pass. Man is subject to the
natural but God can deliver under any circumstance
even if He has to create it just for you. Expect the
best because God can deliver it exactly how you
EXPECT it to show up.

Prophetic Decree

My expectation is from God and God alone. I wait on the Lord and trust totally in His plan for my life. I expect the best and therefore I receive the best. I will not settle or compromise. I expect total delivery on what my heart believes for. I know that God will not fail me.

- PRINCIPLE ELEVEN -
MONEY

I Timothy 6:10

For the love of **money** is the root of all evil: which while some coveted after, they have erred from the faith, and pierced themselves through with many sorrows.

Money is not evil, loving money more than God is. Money is a tool that the Lord will use to bless you and allow you to bless others, even the nations of the earth. This day ask God to give you wisdom to be a great steward of the money that He is bringing into your hand. When you are faithful over the little, He will make you ruler of much more.

Prophetic Decree

I decree that I am money's master and it serves me. I
command money to come into my hands from the
east, west, north and south to fulfill the plans that
God has given me in this earth. I am a money
magnet, and it comes to me frequently and easily. I
have an abundance of money. God uses me as
Kingdom financier to contribute to worthy
Kingdom causes, and to be a blessing in the earth.

- PRINCIPLE TWELVE -
INTEGRITY

I John 2:5

But whoso **keepeth his word**, in him verily is the love of God perfected: hereby know we that we are in him.

You will be known for what you do. You can say a lot, but if your actions contradict what you are speaking then that will be noted. Your talents and gifts may get you in a place, but your character and integrity will keep you there. If you say it, do it and do things that solely bring the Father glory.

Prophetic Decree

I am a person of my Word. What I say is what I actually do. I keep my Word at all cost even when it is inconvenient for me. I am walking out the Word and Will of God to the best of my ability without compromise. I will not cut corners, but will govern my life based on God's infallible Word. I HAVE INTEGRITY!

IMAGE

Genesis 1:26

And God said; Let us make man in our **image**, after our likeness: and let them have dominion over the fish of the sea, and over the fowl of the air, and over the cattle, and over all the earth, and over every creeping thing that creepeth upon the earth.

You are created in the image and likeness of God. Meditate this truth until you see yourself as the Word has described you being righteous, holy, seated in heavenly places, and a joint-heir with Jesus. Many times the devil does maintenance on our image to make us remember the old man. Declare that you are who God says you are and do not accept or answer to any other name.

Prophetic Decree

I am what the Word says I am, I can do what the
Word says I can do, and I can have what the Word
says I can have. I am righteous, I am holy, and I am a
created in the image and likeness of Almighty God. I
refuse any thoughts from Satan from this day forth.
I decree that I am new in Christ Jesus.

- PRINCIPLE FOURTEEN -
INHERITANCE

Proverbs 13:22

A good man leaveth an **inheritance** to his children's children: and the wealth of the sinner is laid up for the just.

Your children and their children do not have to go through the things that you have gone through. One of the most important things is to break generation barriers, by preparing to leave an inheritance of businesses, money, stock, etc. for your children and their children for generations to come. Think generational and not just about you and yours. You can change the course of destiny for your family with this mindset, and cause them to flow into what you left thereby omitting them to start from scratch. Wealth is part of you and your family's inheritance package from the Lord.

Prophetic Decree

I decree a new mindset of generational wealth. I declare that I shall leave an inheritance for my children and their children. I declare the generations that follow me will not have to deal with the struggles of my life, because I have received the wealth of sinners and have invested wisely. I declare blessed shall every generation be after me in Jesus name.

RELATIONSHIPS

Proverbs 18:24

A man that **hath friends** must show himself
friendly: and there is a friend that sticketh closer
than a brother.

Divine relationships must be discerned by the Holy
Spirit. You cannot be in covenant with just anybody.
Make sure there is synergy, honesty, and clear
expectations. Although some relationships are
seasonal, some are for a lifetime and just because it
was seasonal, it does not mean that it was not sent
by God.

Prophetic Decree

I declare that I am able to discern good versus evil in
every relationship. I am in covenant with the right
people. Those alone that God have ordained to
come into my life will be allowed. Lord let the
anointing on my life repel anyone that you did not
send. I receive my covenant connections with joy
and I show myself friendly as we embrace.

- PRINCIPLE SIXTEEN -
INSTINCT

I John 2:20

But ye have an **unction** from the Holy One, and ye know all things.

Trust your gut feeling. It is usually a nudge from the Holy Spirit that is either telling you to go or to stay. Begin to discern and trust that nudge like never before. Those moments come and go, but when acted upon can start something catalytic.

Prophetic Decree

I decree that I have an unction from the Holy Spirit
and I know all things. When He pricks me, I discern
and act upon what He is revealing to me by the
Spirit. My discernment is sharp and I will never be
caught off guard. I am positioned to move forward
in purpose, and when I sense a shift I am able to
adjust and line up with it instinctively.

- PRINCIPLE SEVENTEEN -
DECISIONS

Proverbs 3:5-6

Trust in the LORD with all your heart, and lean not unto thine own understanding. In **all thy ways acknowledge him**, and he shall direct thy paths.

Become a person that can make sound decisions. Indecisiveness is a hindrance. You must make decisions and stick with them. Let the Word of God and the Holy Spirit assist you daily in making those decisions. If you need to back off for a few days then do so; but you must make a sound decision.

Prophetic Decree

I am a sound decision maker. The Holy Spirit gives me unction and I am never confused. In every situation, the Spirit of truth reveals the truth to me every step of the way. I have a sound mind and I am stable in my decision making every time.

- PRINCIPLE EIGHTEEN -
VISION

Habakkuk 2:2

And the Lord answered me, and said, Write the **vision**, and make it plain upon tables, that he may run that readeth it.

As far as you can see, the Lord is able to put it in your hands. It does not cost you anything to imagine and believe God. Let it become clearer and clearer to you. Set aside time today to sit and imagine, then write down what come to your mind. Your inspirations will come from heaven, and as far as you can see, God can do it in your life if you believe. Set goals daily, weekly, monthly, quarterly, and yearly. Monitor and measure your progress. Make adjustments in the areas where things are not moving ahead as you have desired. You may need to change some things, be open to hear from the Lord.

Prophetic Decree

I sit with God daily to get the vision for my day, month, year, for my business, family, and for my life. As I sit I write down what He reveals to me in great detail. I am open to what He shows me, and no matter my level of understanding at the moment is, I write it down. I fully expect to accomplish all goals that I write with excellence.

FIRE

Luke 3:16

John answered, saying unto them all, I indeed
baptize you with water; but one mightier than I
cometh, the latchet of whose shoes I am not worthy
to unloose: he shall baptize you with the Holy Ghost
and with **fire**.

Be not lukewarm, but on fire to fulfill your highest
call in God. If you are called to business, be on fire
about your business, and it will be contagious to all
that hear you speak about it. Let it burn within you
and the passion will stay fresh. Passion and purpose
produces great results.

Prophetic Decree

Lord let your fresh fire burn within me daily. I decree that I am passionate about my purpose and my assignment in the earth. I am not complacent, but energetic and diligent walking out the plan of God. I am on fire, and nothing was cause the flame to go out.

- PRINCIPLE TWENTY -
POSITIONING

Psalm 119:105

Thy word is a lamp unto my feet, and a light unto **my path.**

Make sure that you are positioned to receive what God is delivering to you. Are you in the right place? Do you have the right information? Are you prepared to receive and be promoted if He brings it to you today? If you need to reposition, now is the time; it is never too late or too soon. Be ready because God is faithful. Get in position.

Prophetic Decree

I am divinely positioned in the perfect will of God. I am exactly where I am supposed to be. I have the right information. I am surrounded and connected to the right people. I decree that God leads and guides me daily. His Word is a lamp to my feet and a light to my path, and I am walking it out day by day.

- PRINCIPLE TWENTY-ONE -
REVELATION

Colossians 1:9

For this cause we also, since the day we heard it, do not cease to pray for you, and to desire that ye might be filled with the **knowledge of his will** in all wisdom and spiritual understanding

The knowledge (revelation) of God comes to us as light. It comes suddenly and almost in a flash. It is priceless! Nothing compares to the knowledge that God reveals to us. It consists of things we could not see before, and then He opens our eyes to see, causing us to know with understanding what he is revealing to us. What is revealed to you by God is yours for the taking. He is not just revealing, but when He reveals it, He expects you to grab hold and begin to take responsibility of that revelation.

Prophetic Decree

I decree that I am filled with the knowledge of God's will. He daily gives me wisdom and spiritual understanding. I don't just have natural knowledge but also revelation knowledge. I take full responsibility for all that God reveals to me, and begin to strategically act upon the revealed knowledge. Let there be light!

- PRINCIPLE TWENTY–TWO -
GRACE

II Corinthians 9:8

And God is able to make all **grace** abound toward you; that ye, always having all sufficiency in all things, may abound to every good work

God's unmerited favor is yours! It is made new every day. There is nothing you could have done to earn it. Jesus paid the price, and now all we have to do is to receive it and walk in the grace of God. His grace is sufficient and abounds toward us daily.

Prophetic Decree

I thank you Lord for your grace! I receive it today. I declare that your grace is sufficient for me, and I do not toil in my efforts. I declare that because your grace abounds towards me, I have more than enough to meet the need of every good work that I desire to partake in.

- PRINCIPLE TWENTY–THREE -
THE ANOINTING

Isaiah 10:27

And it shall come to pass in that day, that his burden shall be taken away from off thy shoulder, and his yoke from off thy neck, and the yoke shall be destroyed because of the **anointing**.

The anointing is God's yoke destroying, burden removing power. It allows you to do, what you could not do before with POWER. God's anointing is the enabling force of God that makes all the difference. Without the anointing you will operate in the flesh, but with it, you got the power of God working with you to destroy the works of Satan as Jesus did when He walked the earth as a man.

Prophetic Decree

I decree that I AM anointed! I decree that the anointing upon my life is destroying every yoke and removing every single burden. Because of the anointing I am able to function in my assignment on another level. I experience supernatural results in my life because of the anointing.

- PRINCIPLE TWENTY–FOUR -
MEDITATION

Joshua 1:8

This book of the law shall not depart out of thy mouth; but thou shalt **meditate** therein day and night, that thou mayest observe to do according to all that is written therein: for then thou shalt make thy way prosperous, and then thou shalt have good success.

There is a law of meditation, that what you meditate on you will have produced in your life. God instructs us to meditate His Word and OBSERVE to do what is in it. As we meditate in the Word it guarantees us that we can make our way prosperous and have great success. Meditation brings forth a change in thinking that is in line with the mind of God that can only produce greatness.

Prophetic Decree

I decree that the Bible is my meditation, and I observe and obey what is written in it. As I meditate and I am obedient, I am moving forward and making progress. I am prosperous in my endeavors and I decree that I AM successful.

- PRINCIPLE TWENTY–FIVE -

LOVE

Mark 12:29-31

29 And Jesus answered him, The first of all the commandments is, Hear, O Israel; The Lord our God is one Lord:

30 And thou shalt love the Lord thy God with all thy heart, and with all thy soul, and with all thy mind, and with all thy strength: this is the first commandment.

31 And the second is like, namely this, Thou shalt love thy neighbour as thyself. There is none other commandment greater than these.

Love is the greatest commandment for the believer. We must strive to walk in the agape love of God. This is what sets us apart from anyone else. When we are walking in love, we are expressing and releasing God into our environment or situation.

The demonstration of Love is giving and dying to self. Love never fails, neither try to get its own way. It does not keep an account of a suffered wrong. We must love through it all. By this, God can be glorified and lifted up that He may draw all men unto Him. God is love, and He loved us before we knew Him.

Prophetic Decree

I decree that I am love. I walk in God's agape love with my brothers and sisters in Christ, and with everyone that comes across my path. I purpose in my heart to be a demonstration of God's love. I do not take offense or keep account to anything that has been done to me. God's love is expressed through everything I do and say. I decrease that the greater one may increase in me. I employ the fruit of love and yield to the Holy Spirit, that God can love people through me, with every encounter.

PRAYER

1 Thessalonians 5:17

Pray without ceasing.

Prayer must become a regular part of your day. Bring every request unto the Lord and decree His Word and He shall establish it in your life. Seek Him and you shall find Him. I believe before doing any business, you should transact business with the Father. The time you spend with Him is priceless and that will set the tone for the rest of your day. Pray the Word and pray in tongues in order to build yourself up in your most holy faith. When you pray in the Spirit you are praying the perfect will of God and you connect with the divine source of everything. Your spirit is being strengthened and you shall have a more intimate relationship with the heavenly Father as you do this consistently. You shall grow leaps & bounds.

Prophetic Decree

I seek the Lord daily and I find Him. I set aside time daily to pray and bring my every request to the Lord. I do not put anything before seeking the Father. Praying is a regular part of my life, and I do it without fail. Prayer sets the tone for my day, week and for my life. I am a PRAY-ER, and I pray without ceasing, not only for myself, but I also intercede for others. My prayers are fervent and effectual producing greater works in the earth.

- PRINCIPLE TWENTY–SEVEN -
EXCELLENCE

Daniel 6:3

Then this Daniel was preferred above the presidents and princes, because an **excellent** spirit was in him; and the king thought to set him over the whole realm.

Strive to be a top performer. Go the extra mile to get things not just done but in a special way. Go above and beyond to satisfy the client and even a family member. Have a flow that cannot be denied that you are the best. Be extraordinary and let that become your brand.

Prophetic Decree

I go above and beyond to present the best package, performance and product. I have an excellent spirit and I produce excellent results in all that I do. I do not cut corners or compromise. I give the best of myself and of my services; therefore the best is given unto me. I am known by my excellent, extraordinary delivery and personality.

- PRINCIPLE TWENTY-EIGHT -
THE TEAM

Proverbs 13:20

He that walketh with **wise men** shall be wise: but a companion of fools shall be destroyed.

Teamwork is important for the success of any endeavor. The team must know their strengths and weaknesses and align accordingly. Have team meetings where you can talk and also listen to what the members are saying. Make it work. If it seems impossible –seek God! With Him ALL things are possible.

Prophetic Decree

I am a team player. I work in congruence with my team. God surrounds me with a team and we work together in unity, and all of the gifts flow. We are a well-oiled machine, producing the highest level of teamwork. We value each other, and we let each person demonstrate their perspective gift to the full.

THE BLESSING

Proverbs 10:22

The **blessing** of the Lord, it maketh rich, and he addeth no sorrow with it.

God's blessing is upon your life, and it can produce through you if you put a demand on it. The Blessing removes toil and struggle; it gives you a supernatural flow and performs on a higher level even in the midst of a famine. You have the Blessing on you now!

Prophetic Decree

I invoke the Blessing of the Lord to operate in my life and in all that I do. I thank you Lord the Blessing is making me rich; causing no sorrow or painful toil to be present in my life. I am blessed and the Blessing is in full effect in my life, causing me to prosper in all that I set my hands to.

- PRINCIPLE THIRTY -

THE TONGUE
"WATCH YOUR MOUTH"

Proverbs 18:21

Death and life are in the power of the **tongue**: and they that love it shall eat the fruit thereof.

The Law of confession says that you say exactly what God has said. Never speak out of your mouth, what you do not want to exist in your life. Speak only what you want. God only spoke what He wanted to create. He wanted light therefore He said, "Let there be light, and there was light" (See Genesis 1:3). This is the way you are to function in this earth. Daily, begin to speak ONLY what you want to SEE produced.

Prophetic Decree

I speak the Word only. I am a creator, made in the image and the likeness of God. Therefore I create what I desire by speaking. I only speak words of life, and I expect them to produce the fruit of life. I believe and therefore I speak. I speak and I see manifestation of what I have spoken.

- PRINCIPLE THIRTY–ONE -
CONFIDENCE

1 John 5:14-15

And this is the **confidence** that we have in him, that, if we ask any thing according to his will, he heareth us: And if we know that he hear us, whatsoever we ask, we know that we have the petitions that we desired of him.

Your confidence must be placed on the true and living God. He is the one that covers you on all ends; He does not change and He cannot lie. If He promised it, He can bring it to pass. We must have confidence in Him and in Him alone.

Prophetic Decree

I decree that I am confident in the Lord and in the power of His might. I do not lean on the arm of man, but all hope is in God. I am confident that He that started the good work in me will complete it. I ask according to His Word, and I know that He hears me, and I will possess my inheritance in Jesus name.

- PRINCIPLE THIRTY–TWO -
NO LIMITS

Mark 10:27

And Jesus looking upon them saith, With men it is impossible, but not with God: for **with God all things are possible**.

We have to have a mind that believes that what God has promised to us, is possible. It doesn't matter how it looks or feels at the present time, we must BELIEVE. What is impossible with natural man is POSSIBLE for us and our SUPERNATURAL God. We must believe without adding restrictions. Open your heart and mind to allow God to manifest and create things that have not been discovered.

Prophetic Decree

I BELIEVE GOD! I decree that I take God at His Word. I open up my heart and mind for God Almighty to impart unto to me creative ideas and witty inventions that will change history. I know that all things are possible with God. I believe and receive the ability to create the impossible today.

FAITH

Hebrews 6:12

That ye be not slothful, but followers of them who through **faith** and patience inherit the promises.

You must walk by faith and not by sight. You should not be moved by temporary circumstances. Just as Abraham had to call things that be not as though they were, so should you. (See Romans 4:17) Your faith cannot waver; you must stand until you see the manifestation of the Word in your circumstances. At no point do you speak contrary to what you believe. STAND and your faith will produce!

Prophetic Decree

I declare that I am a person of faith. I call things
that be not as though they were. I stand in faith until
I have taken possession of the promise. I decree that
I do not waver in faith, but holdfast to my
confession of faith with patience. My faith is ever
increasing and this is pleasing to God.

- PRINCIPLE THIRTY–FOUR -
REJECTION

Psalm 118:22

The stone which the builders **refused** is become the head stone of the corner.

It does not matter who tells you no. Keep moving ahead for it is just a matter of time before you get that "YES" and one "YES" is all you need. Do not get down, angry or bitter; just keep moving ahead; for your open door is in front of you! Understand that rejection is a part of life, and don't take it personal.

Prophetic Decree

I am immune to rejection. I do not take it personal
when I am rejected in circumstances or by people. I
continue to move forward knowing this does
not affect my destiny in any way. I rebuke the spirit
of rejection and I receive acceptance from Abba
Father. I thank you Lord that I am accepted in the
Beloved and these things do not affect me or my
esteem in anyway. I am free!

- PRINCIPLE THIRTY–FIVE -
FORGIVENESS

Ephesians 4:32

And be ye kind one to another, tenderhearted, **forgiving** one another, even as God for Christ's sake hath forgiven you.

There is nothing that God will not forgive and you should be the same. No matter how hard it may seem, you must let it go. You will hinder yourself by not forgiving. God knows all about it, so release it to Him that you may be healed and free from all attachments of the past.

Prophetic Decree

I release every person that has ever hurt me and I release myself from any person that I have hurt knowingly or unknowingly. I thank you God for forgiving me for every trespass, having cleansed me from all un-righteousness. I also forgive all for all offenses and repent for holding on to any un-forgiveness in any capacity. I release it this day and separate myself from the curse.

- PRINCIPLE THIRTY–SIX -

CONDEMNATION

Romans 8:1

There is therefore now no **condemnation** to them, which are in Christ Jesus, who walk not after the flesh, but after the Spirit.

No matter what you have done it is under the Blood of Jesus! Do not let the devil tell you otherwise. Your sins have been paid for by the Blood of Jesus, and you are the righteousness of God in Christ Jesus. Declare it & Walk in it!

Prophetic Decree

I declare my past is the past, and it will not affect my
future. I move forward with a clean slate and pure
conscience. The Blood of Jesus has paid the price
for me and I am in right standing with God. I am
purged from all dead works and I am being led into
my destiny by the Holy Spirit every step of the way.

- PRINCIPLE THIRTY–SEVEN -
WHATSOEVER

Mark 11:24

Therefore I say unto you, **What things soever** ye desire, when ye pray, believe that ye receive them, and ye shall have them.

What do you desire? Do not leave this up to chance, and think that things just happen. God needs you to desire, ask, believe and receive! He promises that when you follow this and your desire is aligned with His Word, you shall have those desires. What is stopping you now?

Prophetic Decree

I decree that I know what I want. I make my
requests known to God. I BELIEVE when I pray
that I have received the petition that I am asking of
Him. Whatever I ask in faith, He shall deliver it to
me. I decree my faith moves mountains, produces
wealth and brings forth anything I need and desire.

POWER

Deuteronomy 8:18

But thou shalt remember the Lord thy God: for it is he that giveth thee power to get wealth, that he may establish his covenant which he sware unto thy fathers, as it is this day.

God has given us POWER. He has given us power to produce wealth, and also authority over all of the works of Satan and His cohorts. It is our responsibility to tap into the power that God has already provided for us. We are not waiting on God, He is waiting on us. He has done all He is going to do. Our job is to discover the power within and begin to produce the wealth that is our inheritance.

Prophetic Decree

I decree that the power of God is at work in me and through me. I have tapped into the infinite source of everything and I am producing wealth in my life. God's power in me is in full demonstration, and I am manifesting my inheritance.

- PRINCIPLE THIRTY–NINE -
SETBACKS

Isaiah 54:17

No weapon that is formed against thee shall
prosper; and every tongue that shall rise against thee
in judgment thou shalt condemn.

Challenging situations may occur on the path to
success. As they arise, know that God promised to
deliver you. Remember that the weapons of your
warfare are not carnal and are not to be fought in the
flesh. This is a spiritual war, and you must fight the
good fight of faith regardless of the current
appearance of the situation. God is with you, even in
the midst of the problem. Be mindful to look for the
lesson and the solution, because it was already there
before the problem manifested.

Prophetic Decree

I decree that no weapon formed against me shall prosper, and every tongue that rises against me in judgment shall be condemned. In the midst of adversity I am a rock. I am not moved because I know that this too shall pass. I learn the lesson and quickly find the solution. I declare that I am a problem solver.

- PRINCIPLE FORTY -
HOLY SPIRIT

John 16:7

Nevertheless I tell you the truth; It is expedient for you that I go away: for if I go not away, **the Comforter** will not come unto you; but if I depart, I will send him unto you.

The most important relationship you can have is with the Holy Spirit. He will show you things to come. He will be your Comforter, Counselor, Helper, Advocate, Intercessor, Strengthener, Standby and much more. Develop intimacy with Him. Talk to Him daily, and listen for your divine instructions and assistance. You never have to be confused.

Prophetic Decree

I am in an intimate relationship with the Holy Spirit.
I take time daily to fellowship with Him. I have an
unction from the Holy One and I know all things.
He gives me instructions, wisdom, and comfort in
time of need. I adhere to His counsel and always
have victory.

FULL ARMOR

Ephesians 6:13

Wherefore take unto you the **whole armour** of God, that ye may be able to withstand in the evil day, and having done all, to stand.

We are to put on the armor of the Lord and never take it off. The devil does not know if it is you or Jesus inside. He waits to catch you without your armor and running your mouth, speaking contrary to God's Word. We must stay covered, and constantly speaking the Word. Keep the armor strong and polished and keep your helmet down and your mouth full of faith!

Prophetic Decree

I decree that I not only put on the armor of God,
but I keep it on. I put on the helmet of salvation and
keep the lid down. I put on the breastplate of
righteousness, gird up my loins with TRUTH, and
shod my feet with the preparation of the gospel of
peace. I use the sword of the Spirit with precision
and accuracy.

- PRINCIPLE FORTY–TWO -
YEA & AMEN

II Corinthians 1:20

For all the promises of God in him are **yea**, and in him **Amen**, unto the glory of God by us

Whatever God says in His Word is for you. If it is in the book as a promise, it is available for you to take possession of it. All you need to do is build your faith and take it! The Kingdom of heaven suffers violence, and the violent take it by force.

Prophetic Decree

I believe the promises of God are mine. I build my faith daily and use it to take hold of what God has revealed to me is mine. His promises are mine and I release my faith and walk into the manifestation.

- PRINCIPLE FORTY–THREE -
MENTORS

Proverbs 11:14

Where no counsel is, the people fall: but in the
multitude of counselors there is safety.

It is important to have individuals where you value
the work they have done. You can glean from this
person's life and accomplishments. It can be close up
or from a distance even through books and
teachings. Learn as much as you can from them and
how they got the success that you desire. Their
wisdom can usually keep you from making the same
mistakes they did.

Prophetic Decree

I decree that I have the right people in my life. I have God ordained mentors and counselors that are there to give me instruction, correction, guidance, and wisdom as I need it. I submit unto their authority, and I am obedient to the God directed instructions that are released into my life. I have mentors that pour into me, and I learn from their mistakes, and glean from their accomplishments and wisdom.

- PRINCIPLE FORTY–FOUR -
PRESS

Philippians 3:14

I **press** toward the mark for the prize of the high calling of God in Christ Jesus.

There is a blessing in the pressing. The idea of quitting always comes as you reach the end. The enemy will do everything possible to make you give in, turn coward and faint. However, just as you feel that strain and the pain begin; you catch your second wind and the "PRESS" is on. God is with you, and you are at the brink of your BREAKTHROUGH!

Prophetic Decree

I am an overcomer. I do not give in, become weary, turn coward or give up. I press toward the mark of the high calling of God in Christ Jesus. I know that in my pressing there is a blessing. So I thank you Lord for strength as I proceed to my breakthrough.

- PRINCIPLE FORTY–FIVE -
DILIGENCE

Proverbs 10:4

He becometh poor that dealeth with a slack hand:
but the hand of the **diligent** maketh rich

Diligence is a big key in walking toward success.
Slothfulness cannot be in your plans. You must be
diligent in all that you do and then the Lord will
bless and increase the work of your hands. Take
what you have in front of you serious and be a good
steward over it, no matter the size, the Lord will
multiply your efforts.

Prophetic Decree

I decree that I am diligent in my assignment. In all that the Lord will give me to do, I will do it to the best of my ability. I execute with precision and accuracy every task that I have before me, no matter the size.

- PRINCIPLE FORTY–SIX -
UNDERSTANDING

Proverbs 3:13

Happy is the man that findeth wisdom, and the man that getteth **understanding**.

Having an understanding of a matter creates the ability to perform at a higher level. It is difficult to continue when you do not have understanding. Ask questions if you must, read a book, look up definitions, etc. Do what is necessary to obtain clarity in every circumstance, so that you can move forward with complete truth on the matter; causing you to make the best decisions.

Prophetic Decree

I declare that in all my getting I obtain understanding. I do whatever is necessary to have clarity in any situation that is presented to me. I have understanding therefore I am happy.

- PRINCIPLE FORTY–SEVEN -
THINK

Proverbs 23:7

For as he **thinketh** in his heart, so is he.

Your thoughts produce a belief system. What you believe you will speak. Your life is a manifestation of the words you have spoken. Choose which thoughts you will allow to permeate your mind. What you think is what you will become, and what you are today is a result of the thoughts you had yesterday. Decide what you want for your future and position your thoughts, words and actions to line up.

Prophetic Decree

I declare that I think on things that are true, honest, just, pure, lovely, and of a good report. I focus my thoughts to create the future that I desire to have. I let go of all negativity and facts that are contrary to what I'm believing for. I think on success therefore I AM successful!

- PRINCIPLE FORTY–EIGHT -
EXPLOITS

Isaiah 8:18

Behold, I and the children whom the Lord hath given me are for **signs and for wonders** in Israel from the Lord of hosts, which dwelleth in mount Zion

We are in this world to be a sign and a wonder. We are chosen by God to do greater works than Jesus did. The world should consistently see miracles happen in our lives. It should be the normal for every Christian. We were born to walk in and perform exploits in this earth drawing people unto the Lord to advance the Kingdom.

Prophetic Decree

I decree that I was created for signs, wonder, and miracles. I position myself to flow in the supernatural power of God in all that I do. I walk in exploits, and God uses it to draw people into His Kingdom for further advancement. Exploits are a regular part of my life.

- PRINCIPLE FORTY–NINE -

DISTINCTION

Psalm 139:14

I will praise thee; for I am **fearfully and wonderfully made:** marvelous are thy works; and that my soul knoweth right well.

The Body of Christ and the world should not look the same. There should be a clear difference in the ways and lifestyle of the two. We are to be salt and light as well as healthy, wealthy, and wise. We should be stress free assisting with solving all of the problems in the world. What is your distinctive difference?

Prophetic Decree

I declare that I am set apart. I am peculiar and unique. The world looks at my life and wants to know my God. I operate in my gifts and calling and it brings me before great men. Because I have a distinct call upon my life, all want to use my services and products to move forward in what they are doing.

- PRINCIPLE FIFTY -

CREATIVITY

Genesis 1:27

So God **created** man in his own image, in the image of God created he him; male and female created he them.

There is something on the inside of you that no one can do quite like you. You were born to do it. Others may have something similar, but they do not possess the seed that God planted in you. You must tap into the creative side of your being. You were created in the likeness of your Father, THE CREATOR; therefore you are also a creator. Begin to sit with Him and tap into the creator within.

Prophetic Decree

I tap into the creator within. I am made in the image and likeness of Abba Father and I use words to create. I am a creator. Daily, God downloads me with benefits, creative ideas, and witty inventions to produce wealth, solutions for the world, and bring people into higher levels of prosperity in all areas of life.

- PRINCIPLE FIFTY–ONE -
DESIRE

Psalm 37:4

Delight thyself also in the Lord: and he shall give thee the **desires** of thine heart.

The desire of your heart is what God wants to deliver to you, not just your needs. He gives us all things to richly enjoy and He wants us to live the good life of heaven on earth. We do not have to wait until we get to heaven, we can enjoy His best right here on this earth. Bring your petitions to the Lord and He will give you the desires of your heart.

Prophetic Decree

I believe that God not only wants to give me what I need, but also what I want. I let my desires be known unto to Him and believe I receive the desires of my heart. God's best is flowing into my life today and I will not settle for less.

- PRINCIPLE FIFTY–TWO -
FAITHFULNESS

1 Corinthians 4:2

Moreover it is required in stewards, that a man be found **faithful**.

Faithfulness is required of the Lord in order for Him to trust you with what He has planned for you to rule over. To whom much is given, much is required (See Luke 12:48). Whatever your present assignment is, be faithful. Sometimes God will have you in another man's vision to develop you, your gifts, and faithfulness. He cannot give you much unless you are faithful over the little that is in front of you. Can God trust you?

Prophetic Decree

I decree that I am a faithful person. I understand that where I am now is not my end, and I do my very best in my current situation. I do all that I can to be the best steward I can be with what the Lord has entrusted to me in this season. I declare that as I am faithful in what I now have, that I am ruler over much more in the days ahead, because the Lord can trust me with it. I shall be found faithful in the sight of the Lord.

CONCLUSION

Everything that Abraham got, you get. It is your inheritance. Do not just take some of it and leave the rest. You get it all; wealth, health, wisdom, family, education, etc. It is all yours and do not settle for anything less.

God gave you your brain to THINK. Take time each day to do this by sitting down with no noise or distractions. Write down what comes to you because daily the Lord gives us new ideas, revelation, and solutions to problems. The decisions you to make today, will be the reflection of the results that you will have in your tomorrow.

God has given each of us the POWER to get WEALTH. It is our responsibility to tap into the CREATIVITY that is WITHIN and begin to PRODUCE the GOOD LIFE, which He ORDAINED for us before the foundation of the world. In the Bible, Deuteronomy 8:18 says, "But thou shalt remember the Lord thy God: for it is he that giveth thee power to get wealth, that he may establish his covenant which he sware unto thy fathers, as it is this day."

What are you doing with what He gave you? Change can be hard, but when you know what you are doing is not working, you must purpose in your heart to make changes, and have an action plan that will bring that decision into full manifestation. Let the past go and ask God for new direction so that you may start fresh.

Philippians 3:13-14

13 Brethren, I count not myself to have apprehended: but this one thing I do, forgetting those things which are behind, and reaching forth unto those things which are before,

14 I press toward the mark for the prize of the high calling of God in Christ Jesus.

The last thing I want to leave you with is to value your TIME. You must decide how you spend it. While writing this book, I had to say no to a lot of temptations, and I had to be determined to finish the book. I knew that if I wanted to play hard later that would have to work smart now. Time is the only thing that you do not get back. Watching television, spending time with your family and other people etc. should not consume most of your time. Yes we love family and enjoy doing those things, but producing your God given purpose should be your first priority.

Continue to walk in love, but let people know that you are working on something. God placed you here for such a time as this, and there is work for you to complete. Prioritize! Discipline Yourself! Focus! Take Action!

PRAYER OF SALVATION

God loves you just the way you are. He sent His only begotten Son Jesus to die for you and I. Say this prayer below to accept Him into your heart that He can begin to lead you into the destiny that He has waiting for you.

Please pray this prayer:

Father God, I come to you now, just as I am. You know my life; you know how I have lived. Forgive me Lord I repent of my sins. I believe that Jesus Christ is the Son of God and that He died for my sins. I believe that on the third day He was raised from the dead. Lord Jesus, I ask you now to come inside of my heart, live your life in me and through me from this day forth I belong to you. Jesus be Lord over my life. I believe and receive you right now in Jesus name, amen.

BAPTISM OF THE HOLY SPIRIT

The Baptism of the Holy Spirit is a gift from God. It is vital to the life of a believer in that the Holy Spirit comes upon you and endows you with power. The evidence of this infilling that is available to every believer is the manifestation of speaking in tongues.

Please pray this prayer:

Father, I ask You in the name of Jesus to fill me with the Holy Spirit. I step into the fullness of power that I desire in the name of Jesus. I confess that I am a Spirit filled Christian and as I yield my vocal organs, I expect to speak in tongues, for the Spirit gives me utterance in the name of Jesus.

Scripture Reference:
Acts 1:8
Acts 2:4
Acts 10:44-46
John 14:16-17
Luke 11:13
1 Corinthians 14:2-15
Jude 1:20

ABOUT THE AUTHOR

Tiffany K. Jordan is a visionary leader with prophetic insight to empower and equip people to walk in purpose and successfully reach their destiny. She is known as an intercessor, entrepreneur, life coach, advisor, and mentor. Her anointing divinely positions people into their God given assignments in the Body of Christ and in the world, to maximize potential and dominate in their sphere of influence.

Tiffany answered the call into ministry while working for a prestigious law firm in downtown Chicago. She started a Bible study on the lunch hour, which led many to develop more intimate relationships with God where signs, wonders and miracles followed the Word. The Lord led Tiffany to resign from her assignment at the Law Firm and begin full time preparation and service of ministry.

Tiffany graduated from Living Word School of Ministry and Missions and is licensed by Faith Ministerial Alliance. She is also a graduate of the Joseph Business School of Entrepreneurship.

Tiffany currently is the Prayer Ministry Coordinator at Living Word Christian Center, pastored by Dr. Bill Winston and has been a member since 2003.

Tiffany is the founder of Tiffany Jordan Ministries Inc. (TJM), which is a 501(c) 3 organization. She is an advisor to leaders, assists in strategic planning for visionaries, and provides spiritual guidance with the wisdom of God. She is the CEO of Covenant Connection Corporation, a consulting firm that provides Kingdom solutions for Marketplace dominion. She preaches and teaches the Word of God, leading many to accept Jesus Christ as Lord, and equips them to become effective citizens of the Kingdom of God. Tiffany resides in Chicago, Illinois and is the mother of two daughters, Shondasia and Corinthia.

Contact Tiffany Jordan Online:

www.CovenantConnectionCorp.com

www.TiffanyJordanMinistries.com

www.facebook.com/TiffanyJordanMinistries

www.Facebook.com/CovenantConnection

www.Facebook.com/tiffany.jordan.96343

www.twitter.com/tjmi1

Postal Mail:

380 East St. Charles #231
Lombard, IL 60148

30996613R00076

Made in the USA
Charleston, SC
02 July 2014